THE CROMER LIFEBOA

THE NORFOLK SHIPWRECK A

Cromer was not a large p ne beginning of the nineteenth c own but also a shipping centre of ourishing trade, though the town had no ships voyaged all round the British coast as well n the open beach of their home port.

So there was already a seafaring tradition in the town when, in October 1804, a notice appeared in the Norwich Mercury inviting "Those Gentlemen, Visitants and Inhabitants of Cromer and the neighbourhood, who wish to encourage the establishment of Life Boat" to meet at the local hotel to lay plans for the opening of a lifeboat station.

Following that meeting a committee of eighteen prominent local people, headed by Lord Suffield and Colonel Harbord, was appointed to raise a subscription and order a lifeboat from Henry Greathead of South Shields, who had earlier built a number of non-self-righting lifeboats for various stations, including two in Suffolk. Nearly £700 had been subscribed by the following January and the lifeboat was obtained, though there does not seem to have been enough money forthcoming at the time for the building of other boats "to provide a more general safe-guard along the coast from Sherringham to Yarmouth than one boat admits of." It was to be several years before other boats appeared on the Norfolk coast.

Records of the early work of this first lifeboat are scanty, but it is known that she was in use during a nor'-easterly gale in November 1810, when the brig *Anna* of Sunderland came ashore between Cromer and Runton. When news came to Cromer of the wreck the fishermen quickly launched the lifeboat and rowed her strongly towards the stranded vessel, saving fourteen men and a woman passenger.

It was not long after that rescue that the Cromer lifeboat committee, which had also been quick as well as far-sighted in making use of Captain George Manby's line-throwing mortar, decided to station a lifeboat at Mundesley as soon as the necessary money could be obtained. A beach boat was fitted up as a temporary lifeboat for the village, and eventually a small lifeboat costing £130 was built at Sunderland for that station.

Cromer's second lifeboat, 1830-1858. The 'saucer' shape is distinctive, with the substantial cork band. The oars pulled against thole pins. (P A Vicary)

The third Lord Suffield, who like his predecessors at Gunton Park was a leading member of the Cromer lifeboat committee, saw the horrors of shipwreck at close quarters one day in the autumn of 1823, even to the extent of having a corpse washed ashore at his feet while helping to save the crew of a ship off Bacton, or so it is said. The experience made such a very strong impression on him that the next day he sent his servant to the Lord Lieutenant of Norfolk proposing the institution of "an association for preserving the lives of shipwrecked mariners on the whole line of the coast of Norfolk."

It might, therefore, be said that it was the activities of the Cromer lifeboat committee that brought about the formation of the Norfolk Association for Saving the Lives of Shipwrecked Mariners, the first county association to be formed for such a purpose in Britain.

Yet just a few years before the Cromer lifeboat had been said to have been unemployed for a long time, and there was the suggestion that she should be sent to a station where she was more likely to be used. Only the memory of her success in 1810 had persuaded the committee to keep her at Cromer. The boat did go to a new station, at Wells, in 1830, but only because she had been replace by a new boat of an improved type built by Robson, a

Shields boatbuilder, A model of this boat in the Maritime Museum for East Anglia at Yarmouth shows that she had tubes in the bottom to carry away any water that came on board, with a deck above water level, unlike her predecessor.

The boat was in action on October 18th 1839, when a collier brig, the *Achilles* of South Shields, was seen to the eastward with her mainmast and foretopmast carried away. The lifeboatmen managed with considerable difficulty to get her into the roadstead and anchored her off Cromer, and then brought the crew ashore. Next day they went back at first light and attempted to pump the vessel out, but the sea was "making a passage above her" and in spite of the lifeboatmen's efforts she went down about noon. One of the Cromer men, Henry Nockels, was washed overboard, but fortunately he grabbed a rope and was hauled on board; another, Capt Francis Pank, one of the local master mariners who had his home in Cromer's High Street, was injured when he fell between the lifeboat and the brig.

Such trouble did not deter the crew when a vessel appeared off the town with a signal of distress flying just a few days later. It was the Dutch galliot *Elizabeth*, which was in a sinking state after having been driven across the North Sea by a severe storm, which struck when she was about to enter her home port of Harlingen at the end of a twenty-day voyage from Memel in the Baltic, with timber. The lifeboat reached her just as she ran ashore on the beach, and in spite of the heavy seas took off the crew of seven. The rescued Dutchmen caused quite a lot of amusement, and embarrassment, by showing their joy and relief by kissing each other and the bystanders indiscriminately as they stepped ashore from the lifeboat.

During the 1840s the Cromer lifeboats made several appearances at the Yarmouth North Roads Regattas, of which a trial of lifeboats formed part. The crews of those days seem to have thought nothing of rowing to Yarmouth and back for such an event; the lifeboat was not then a sailing craft.

The Norfolk Shipwreck Association (as the NASLSM was usually known for short) was always in need of money, and in 1845, when the first gathering of lifeboats was held at Yarmouth, it was remarked that "though crews are never wanting, subscriptions frequently are." Perhaps that was one of the reasons for the local lifeboat establishment getting into a parlous state in the 1850s.

A correspondent in the Norwich Mercury in 1857 complained that the Cromer lifeboat had "not been out of its house for three and a half years up to last August, and that it was then only taken out at the earnest wish of some of the visitors staying there, and the expense subscribed by them."

The same correspondent had more comments to make later that year after the Cromer fishermen had refused to man the lifeboat during a storm in October. "The lifeboat has not been used for a considerable time, so I am told, that it might be a question whether she was seaworthy," he remarked, adding that there "was no organisation amongst the men, no head, none of the unity which gives forces and direction..."

There was, apparently, no regular crew and no coxswain.

THE LIFEBOAT INSTITUTION

At the end of the year the Royal National Lifeboat Institution took over the Norfolk lifeboat stations, and in the course of the following year sent a 34ft self-righting lifeboat to Cromer to "replace the old lifeboat there, now worn out."

According to RNLI records this boat was launched on services six times and saved five lives in the ten years she wa at the station before being replaced by a more up-to-date self-righting lifeboat which was presented to the RNLI by Mr Benjamin Bond Cabbell, who also paid for the building of the lifeboat house which stands at the foot of the Gangway.

The new boat, which took the name of her donor, performed some good work, in 1869 saving eighteen people from an American ship which was wrecked off the town. In October 1883, the lifeboatmen found that they could make no headway against a gale and heavy seas and were unable to render assistance to the *Alpha* of Sunderland, which came ashore at Cromer after having shipped a heavy sea when north-east of the Dudgeon.

An extract from the entry in the station log for April 9th, 1868, referring to the 'Agenoria' (see page 5). Coxswain Bob Allen has signed with his 'mark'.

DATES AND CIRCUMSTANCES OF THE CASE.

Wind N.E. Gale

A Schooner observed at 7 this morning about fo[ur] miles to the Northward of Cromer riding at anchor, with f[ore] topmast gone (& sails) she slipped her anchor about 9 o'cl[ock] & attempted to weather Cromer, but being light Vessel, wa[ter] logged - (& lost fore topmast) or otherwise disabled, it was a[n] impossibility for her to do, & when abreast of Cromer hard u[p] & ran for shore

QUERIES.	ANSWERS AND REMARKS.
1. Name of Vessel, and where belonging to? . . . 1.	Agenoria Lowestoft

Bob his X mark Allen — COXSWAIN-SUPERINTENDENT.

The 'Benjamin Bond Cabbell' on the beach in front of the schooner 'Agenoria', April 1868. The schooner later broke up where she lay.

The crew of the *Alpha* were eventually rescued by means of a line taken off to the wreck by a coastguardsman, John Davis, but the lifeboat's failure created something of a scandal locally. There were those who contended that the *Benjamin Bond Cabbell*, a ten-oared boat with a length of 34ft and a beam of 8ft 8in, was quite unsuitable for the conditions at Cromer, and they put their views strongly at a meeting held the following week to decide what should be done.

The coxswain, James Davies, and some of the crew wanted a bigger boat with more oars and more curvature in the keel to enable it to turn more easily, but others were determined to have one similar to the one they had had before 1858. The model now in the Maritime Museum for East Anglia at Yarmouth was produced to show just what they meant.

A whole series of meetings and discussions over the next two or three months resulted in the order being given to Beeching's at Yarmouth to build a 35ft boat with a 10ft beam which was in its general design similar to those boats in use at the mouth of the River Tyne and which satisfied the requirements of the Cromer fishermen who were to man her.

Oddly enough, she was also a reversion to the type which had been emphatically rejected on the Suffolk coast some eighty years before; all too clearly it was a case of one man's meat being another's poison.

The new boat, given the same name as her self-righting predecessor, carried out some useful work at Cromer during her eighteen-year period of service. One of her launches was made on the well-known occasion when

Above: *The RNLI lifeboat 'Benjamin Bond Cabbell'. Of the self-righting type, she rowed five oars each side. She was donated by Benjamin Bond Cabbell.*
Below *The 'Benjamin Bond Cabbell' on the beach. Her failure to launch to the 'Alpha' in 1883 led to her replacement. (P A Vicary)*

the excursion paddle-steamer *Victoria* grounded on the Church Rock in August 1888, but most of her work was done during the winter months and in much less pleasant conditions. She was launched on service thirteen times and saved 26 lives, compared with the first *Benjamin Bond Cabbell*'s record of nine launches and 31 lives saved.

Those figures pale into insignificance beside the record of the boat which took over at Cromer in 1902 and served there for nearly thirty years, the *Louisa Heartwell.* She performed 115 launches and was responsible for the rescue of no fewer that 195 people, a record only surpassed at Cromer by the boat which served at the No 1 station there during the 1939-45 War.

It was not only the lifeboats that gave long service, of course. Coxswain James Davies was a member of the Cromer crew for 30 years. spending 21 of them as coxswain, and on his death the crew chose his son, young James, to succeed him; the son was a member of the crew for nearly as long as his father.

On the arrival of the *Louisa Heartwell,* however, James Harrison was appointed coxswain, with young Henry Blogg as second coxswain. When James Harrison resigned because of illness in 1909 he had been in the crew for no less than 41 years, but this impressive record was easily beaten by his successor as coxswain, Henry Blogg, who was in charge of the boat for 38 years and served in the lifeboat for well over half a century.

COXSWAIN HENRY BLOGG

Henry Blogg is probably the most famous of all lifeboatmen, for he became a legend in his own lifetime. He won the Gold Medal of the RNLI three times, being only the second man in the history of the lifeboat service to do so (the first was Sir William Hilary, the founder of the RNLI), and the Silver Medal four times; and he also gained the George Cross and the British Empire Medal.

He won his first Gold Medal in the *Louisa Heartwell* when in 1917 eleven men were rescued from the Swedish steamer *Fernebo,* which had been blown in half by a mine during a terrific gale. Two other members of the crew gained the Silver Medal and the rest were awarded Bronze Medals for this service, which was marked in a high degree by tenacity, physical endurance, unwavering courage and skilful seamanship. The Cromer lifeboat had already that same day saved 16 from the Greek steamer *Pyrin.*

Lifesaving work in a pulling and sailing lifeboat in such conditions as were experienced that day certainly called for a very high degree of physical

The 'Esras' ashore on the west beach, 1901. Although the lifeboat was at the scene, the rocket brigade brought the crew of the 'Esras' ashore. (Randall/Salter)

effort, both in getting the boat afloat and it getting to the scene of the wreck; the crew might be wet through, chilled to the marrow and well-nigh exhausted before even reaching the stage of being able to effect a rescue. Sometimes, indeed, it proved impossible to get the boat afloat at all; such a situation occurred in 1901 when the Norwegian vessel *Esras* came ashore at East Runton after having spent the night on the Haisbro' Sands, the work of lifesaving having to be left to the rocket brigades from Cromer and Sheringham.

Only the introduction of motor lifeboats and the building of a new boathouse on the end of Cromer pier, from which the lifeboat could be launched down a slipway, made it possible for launching to be carried out in almost any conditions, though great courage, stamina and skill were still needed on

The second 'Benjamin Bond Cabbell' lifeboat. Rowing seven oars each side, the type was called the 'Cromer' class. (Randall/Salter)

The second 'Benjamin Bond Cabbell' being dragged along the promenade to the 'Esras', ashore on the west beach. (Poppyland Collection)

the part of every member of her crew. However, now as then, the lifeboat could not re-house at the pierhead in rough conditions, and after a service launch would have to go into Yarmouth harbour.

It was in 1923 that the Royal National Lifeboat Institution sent the first motor lifeboat for the pierhead boathouse, from them on known as the Number One boat, whilst that on the beach became Number Two. She was the first of four boats to be provided for Cromer under the legacy of Mr Henry Francis Bailey, of Brockenhurst in Hampshire, and was a 46ft 6in boat of the Norfolk and Suffolk type, costing nearly £11,000.

Though the builders, J S White of Cowes, had put very good work into her, and she was a very fine boat, the *H F Bailey* did not prove suitable for the

The second 'Benjamin Bond Cabbell', probably on a Lifeboat Day, as the crew have their red caps. It is thought to be the Hon. Secretary, Henry Sandford, in the stern.

Three photographs of the 'Louisa Heartwell', a lifeboat regarded very highly by the Cromer crew. She is also featured on the back cover of this booklet. We are indebted to two photographers, Philip Vicary and H H Tansley, for many of the lifeboat pictures from early in the century. These three are by the latter.

work she was expected to do in the Cromer area. Coxswain Blogg's rather blunt statement was that "Her bows don't make a hole big enough for her stern to go through!" After she had made only three service launches, saving twelve lives, she was transferred to Gorleston, where she spent the next fifteen years under the new name of *John and Mary Meiklam of Gladswood.* At Gorleston she was a very successful and well-liked boat.

The boat which took her place at Cromer was a 45ft Watson type with twin screws; this boat also took her predecessor's name. In her, Coxswain Blogg carried out several of his most famous and most daring rescues, including the saving of fifteen men from the forepart of the oil tanker *Georgia* which had broken in two when a North Sea gale flung her into the Haisbro' Sands in November 1927. The Cromer lifeboatmen had already spent the night standing by the stern section of the tanker, from which fifteen of the crew had been taken by the steamer *Trent*; when they were called to help those on the forepart, already stranded there for 36 hours.

The first of the motor lifeboats, the 'H F Bailey'. The wheel can clearly be seen, as at that time there was no cabin on the boat. (H H Tansley)

Just as the *H F Bailey* approached the wreck one of the cargo tanks burst open under the pounding of the waves, allowing the oil it contained to spread over the sea. That oil gave Coxswain Blogg just the chance he needed, and he seized it with both hands. Taking advantages of the relatively smooth area created by the oil, he took the lifeboat close in to give the men on the *Georgia's* bridge a chance to jump. Some were about to do so when a heavy sea caught the lifeboat, swung her completely round and

The stern of the 'Georgia', which stayed visible on the sands for long enough for photographers to visit. (H H Tansley)

flung her stern hard against the steel side of the wreck, doing considerable damage.

It was still possible to bring her alongside. Heaving lines were thrown to the men on the *Georgia's* bridge and ropes made fast to hold the lifeboat in position. One by one they leapt into the boat, and then as the lines were cut the lifeboat began to turn away.

Just at that moment a heavy sea caught the lifeboat, carrying her onto the *Georgia's* bulwarks. Motor mechanic Bob Davies did not wait for orders; he slammed the engines into reverse, and the lifeboat drew clear, though not without severe damage.

Blogg won the second service clasp to the Gold Medal and each member of the crew received the Bronze Medal for that most hazardous of rescues, in which the Gorleston and Southwold lifeboats were also involved.

The second 'H F Bailey' which carried out the service to the 'Georgia' (P A Vicary)

The following year the *H F Bailey* was sent to a boatyard for permanent repairs to the damage sustained in the service to the *Georgia* and her place was taken by one of the first twin-engined 45ft 6in Watson boats, named *H F Bailey II.*

Once again, the Cromer crew and their coxswain did not like the new boat, and when the *H F Bailey* left the boatyard in 1929, it was to return to her old station, the *H F Bailey II* being sent off to another station under another name.

THE *SEPOY*

It is hard to say which was the most famous of Henry Blogg's many rescues, performed in peace and war, but the service to the spritsail barge *Sepoy* in 1933 certainly became better known than others because it was performed within sight of the town of Cromer and at least two photographers were on hand to record the scene. This operation conclusively proved the supremacy of the motor lifeboat, because the *H F Bailey* took off the two men from the barge after the pulling and sailing No 2 boat, the *Alexandra,* had failed in several rescue attempts.

The *Sepoy* was only one of several vessels in trouble off the Norfolk coast in a severe easterly gale on December 13th 1933. The *H F Bailey* was originally called out to the aid of another barge, the *Glenway,* which had gone ashore at Happisburgh, and was on her way to Gorleston when the *Sepoy* began drifting into shallow water off Overstrand.

There was no radio with which to recall the lifeboat, and with the *H F Bailey* heading away from the scene of the wreck, attempts were made to get the *Alexandra* afloat. Twice she was launched; and twice the seas flung her back onto the beach. When it became obvious that even if the boat were launched from the foot of the Gangway, close to the No 2 lifeboathouse (now the lifeboat museum), it would be impossible to row her to the wreck, a hundred men and women rallied to the lifeboat carriage dragropes and hauled the *Alexandra* half a mile along the wind-lashed beach.

Meanwhile, the Honorary Secretary at Cromer telephoned his counterpart at Gorleston asking for a message to be given to Coxswain Blogg, telling him to return as quickly as possible. The Gorleston secretary realised that minutes were precious and sent his own boat to meet the *H F Bailey*, and if for any reason the Cromer boat could not return the *John and Mary Meiklam of Gladswood* could sail to the aid of the men on the barge. The *John and Mary Meiklam* set out and signalled the message to Blogg.

R N
L I

One of a series of dramatic photos by Philip Vicary of the Sepoy rescue. The 'Alexandra' is on the beach as a line is fired. The photo filled the front cover of the Daily Mirror the next day.

The rocket lifesaving apparatus was brought into action while the *Alexandra* was being dragged along the beach, and after three rockets had been flung aside by the wind a fourth took the line right across the barge's deck. The *Alexandra* was eventually launched, and her crew pulled mightily at the oars in an attempt to get the boat alongside the barge, which was drifting slowly westwards.

Wind and sea proved too much for them, however, and the lifeboat was swept down past the barge's stern, fouling the rocket line as she went. The line parted as the lifeboat was flung back onto the beach.

Opposite- Top left: *H F Bailey ON670* ***Top right:*** *H F Bailey ON694 (H H Tansley)* ***Middle:*** *H F Bailey II ON714* ***Bottom:*** *H F Bailey ON777 (P A Vicary)*

'The Ruby and Arthur Reed II' and the inshore lifeboat 'Spirit of Round Table' on exercise. The photos show Honorary Secretary Jim Smith receiving a launch request, winchman Ted Luckin knocking out the launch pin and Cox'n Richard Davies supervising the recovery of the lifeboat. Other photos show the procedure for letting out the veering lines which hold the lifeboat steady as it is recovered, and the boathouse crew dragging the winch wire out. Once the wire is attached, the green flag signals that the winch can begin hauling the boat back into the boathouse. (Poppyland Photos)

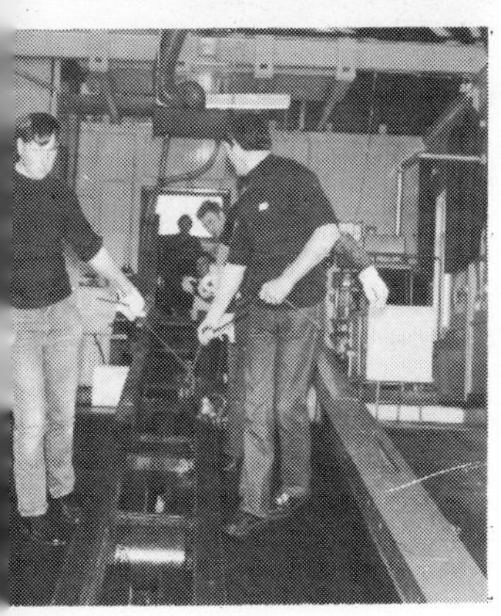

It was mid-afternoon when the *H F Bailey* arrived on the scene and the crew of the barge had already spent several hours in the rigging. The seas were breaking right over the barge's decks as the tide rose, but the two men heard the shouts from the shore and got ready to be taken off.

It was only by driving the bows of the lifeboat right up on the barge's almost submerged deck that Coxswain Blogg was able to take the two men off. With his own crew wet through and tired out, and the rescued men in poor shape, he decided to beach the lifeboat at Cromer rather than to make for Yarmouth harbour; there was no possibility of getting the boat onto the slip in such conditions.

The year before Blogg had been awarded the Silver Medal for the rescue of 30 men and a dog from the Italian steamer *Monte Nevoso*; he gained a second service clasp to that medal for the rescue of the two men from the *Sepoy*, while each member of the *H F Bailey*'s crew received the thanks of the Institution on Vellum, and so did Bob Davies, who had been given charge of the *Alexandra*.

It had obviously been a wise precaution to leave the pulling and sailing boat at Cromer as No 2 boat after the coming of the motor lifeboat; the need for a second motor lifeboat seemed no less obvious after the wreck of the *Sepoy*, and in 1934 the Royal National Lifeboat Institution sent a smaller motor lifeboat, the 35ft 6in Liverpool type boat *Harriot Dixon* to take the place of the *Alexandra* in the boathouse at the foot of the Gangway. In 1935, the fourth lifeboat named *H F Bailey* came to the pierhead station. She was destined to be the busiest of the Cromer lifeboats, being launched on service 128 times and saving 518 lives.

WARTIME SERVICE

During the 1939-45 war both the Cromer lifeboats were to do a great deal of excellent work, a good deal of it necessitated by the demands of war. When hostilities broke out in September 1939, the Cromer lifeboatmen had already had a taste of modern warfare, having been called to the Spanish steamer *Cantabria* when she was attacked by the Spanish insurgent raider *Nadir* not far off the Norfolk coast on November 2nd 1938. In this, as in other ways, the Spanish Civil War gave a foretaste of what was to come.

The first wartime service had nothing to do with enemy action, however, for on October 9th 1939, the *H F Bailey* was launched to the aid of the Greek steamer *Mount Ida* which had gone aground on the Ower Sand. In a very fine but extremely difficult rescue, Coxswain Blogg and his crew saved all 29 men from the Greek ship, though one man died later in Cromer Hospital from injuries he received when he was crushed between the lifeboat and the ship's side. Henry Blogg gained the third service clasp to his Silver Medal that day, while Second Coxswain J J Davies was awarded the second service clasp to the Bronze Medal and mechanic H W Davies and assistant mechanic J W Davies received clasps to their Bronze Medals, the other eight crew members receiving the Institution's thanks inscribed on vellum.

Wartime service for the lifeboats was rather different to the peacetime way of going about things. Under normal circumstances, the Hon Secretary was responsible for the launch of a lifeboat, but the boats also operated under naval control during the period of hostilities. The maroons were not sounded to call the crew, the summons coming by telephone or messenger, and once at sea there were fewer lightships and navigation lights, and restrictions on radio talk. A gap was blown in the pier at Cromer in case of invasion, but no sooner was it made than it had to be bridged so that the lifeboatmen could reach the No 1 lifeboat. On the positive side was the co-operation between lifeboats, RAF high-speed rescue launches and search aircraft.

Long hours during wartime were spent in often fruitless searches, while on other occasions incidents occurred very close to the lifeboat station. It took only eighteen minutes from launching for the *H F Bailey* to pick up the crew of five from a ditched Wellington bomber on 26th July 1943, and on other occasions it was quicker for the lifeboatmen to use their own crab boats. The crew of a B-17 bomber were saved in this way on the same afternoon of the 26th. The longest job was that of salvage work on the *Teddington,* which stranded after being set on fire by enemy aircraft. The *H F Bailey* took out firemen and pumps, cutting equipment and stores, and, sharing the task with the *Harriot Dixon,* the lifeboats were involved from 17th September to 6th November 1941.

CONVOY 559

However, two events stand out in the history of the Cromer lifeboats during the Second World War. The first was the amazing occurrence of 6th August 1941. Convoy 559, avoiding the man-made hazards of war, set onto the Haisbro' Sands in a nor'nor'westerly gale and six vessels found themselves hard aground. The seas on the Sands began their merciless pounding while screws tore at the water to no avail. It was eight in the morning before news reached Cromer of the night's events.

An hour and 40 minutes after launch the Cromer No 1 lifeboat reached the scene, finding the vessels on the southern end of the Sands. Rescue had

Left: Henry Blogg, cox'n 1909-1947 (P A Vicary). Right: Six Cromer cox'ns - James Davies 1872-93, John James Davies 1893-1902, James Harrison 1902-09, Jack Davies, bowman and second cox'n to Blogg, Henry Davies 1947-76, Lewis Harrison, last cox'n of the Number 2 Station.

already begun, with a whaler from an escorting destroyer having taken off most of the crew of the steamer *Taara*. Early rescue attempts cost the lives of twelve men and the Admiralty report states that the whaler had performed its rescue "in steep breaking seas in which it was to be expected that no boat could live."

Blogg, at the helm of the *H F Bailey*, went first to the *Oxshott*, which had only her upperworks showing. At first there seemed to be no sign of life, but then the lifeboatmen saw survivors, roped together. Going alongside was evidently impossible, so Blogg rammed the lifeboat into a wedge-shaped opening in her upperworks. He rammed her in again and again, right over the decks of the *Oxshott* until all sixteen men were aboard the lifeboat.

The 'Harriot Dixon' being launched for the first time with the aid of a tractor in February 1938. Tractor launching had been pioneered at Hunstanton. (P A Vicary)

Turning to the French steamer *Gallois,* which was still above water, the *H F Bailey* took aboard 31 men by rope or jumps from deck to deck. The Cromer No 2 boat, *Harriot Dixon,* then arrived and 2nd Coxswain Jack Davies transferred to her, being familiar with the scene. Survivors were transferred from the *H F Bailey* to a destroyer before she made for the *Deerwood.* Again the lifeboat went over submerged decks to pluck off 19 men before running alongside the *Paddy Hendly* for 22 more. Meanwhile the *Harriot Dixon* rescued eight from the *Taara* whilst the Gorleston lifeboat *Louise Stephens* saved 23 from the Scottish steamer *Aberhill.* The *Harriot Dixon* transferred her survivors to a destroyer before returning to station, while the *H F Bailey* continued to Yarmouth harbour, checking a wrecked trawler on the way.

This was to be the occasion of Henry Blogg's third service clasp to his Gold Medal and the receipt of the British Empire Medal, while Jack Davies and Coxswain Johnson of Gorleston received Silver Medals. Second Coxswain Leslie Harrison of the *Harriot Dixon* received a second clasp to his Bronze Medal, as did motor mechanic 'Swank' Davies, along with the mechanics of the *Harriot Dixon* and the *Louise Stephens.* The thanks of the Institution on Vellum went to all the other crew members. Following the rescue the flag-officer at Yarmouth signalled "I have been instructed by the Commander-in-Chief, Nore, to convey his sincere congratulations and admiration for the superb seamanship displayed..."

THE *ENGLISH TRADER*

The second outstanding event of the war was the service to the *English Trader,* aground on the Hammond Knoll, ten weeks after the convoy incident. Five men had drowned and 44 remained as the *H F Bailey* arrived at about 11.30am, after a journey of nearly three and a half hours. Confused seas swept over the hull of the stricken vessel and Blogg decided to stand by until slack water at 4pm. From the deeper and less troubled water an attempt looked possible using a rocket line. The lifeboat closed the *English Trader* but to no avail.

At about 2.15pm another attempt was made. Blogg was for waiting, but the younger crew, with the success of the convoy behind them, though it worth a try. Moving again into the confused seas, the lifeboat had to turn broadside.

Before it was possible to complete the turn, a wall of water overwhelmed the lifeboat. Survivors from the *English Trader* later said they had seen the keel of the lifeboat, but in Blogg's words "Providence" righted the boat. Five lifeboatmen were in the water, two clung to the guardrails. Crewman W H Davies took the wheel and steered for his coxswain and second cox. The five men were all then brought aboard, but signalman 'Boy Primo' Allen had spent 25 minutes in the water and died after a few minutes. Blogg headed for Yarmouth.

On her journey the *H F Bailey* passed the *Louise Stephens* on her way to the *English Trader.* The Gorleston boat was to get a line aboard only for it to be broken and for darkness to defeat her crew.

The exhausted Cromer men went to the Shipwrecked Sailors' Home and a car set out from Cromer with a replacement signalman. Three hours before daylight the *H F Bailey* left Yarmouth Harbour and 20 minutes after dawn had broken, she was back with the *English Trader.* The storm had abated and the lifeboat was able to go alongside without great difficulty, the vessel's railings now being almost alongside the lifeboat's deck. The 44 survivors were in Yarmouth before noon.

Henry Blogg was awarded the fourth service clasp to his Silver Medal and each of the other ten members of the crew involved in the earlier part of the service, including 'Boy Primo' Allen, was awarded either the Bronze Medal or a clasp to the Bronze Medal already held. Mrs Allen was granted a pension by the Institution on the same scale as if her husband had been a seaman in the Royal Navy who had died in action.

HENRY 'SHRIMP' DAVIES

The end of the war brought to Cromer a new No 1 lifeboat. The *Millie Walton* came in December 1945, originally destined for the Isle of Man. A Watson lifeboat, she had a new midships steering position, which the crew found to their liking. Thus the lifeboat remained at Cromer, and was officially renamed the *Henry Blogg* in 1948.

Her namesake made his last lifeboat voyage under the new coxswain, Henry 'Shrimp' Davies, on 4th September 1948, to the steam trawler *Balmoral.* Henry Blogg was then 71 years old, with 53 years service in lifeboats. He was and is the holder of most awards by the RNLI.

'Shrimp' Davies' qualities were to be tested to the full in the service to the *Francois Tixier* of Dunkirk on July 8th 1948. Captain Ollivier was taking his vessel from Goole to Rouen when its cargo of coal shifted. The lifeboat *Henry Blogg* launched at 11am into a very rough gale, with the wind north by west. The wreck was reached at 12.15pm, four miles north of Sheringham, by which time she was listing heavily to port. Eleven men had been brought on board the lifeboat when the stricken vessel began to sink. Ropes were chopped away, and one man was pulled clear, four more being rescued from a raft. Throughout the rescue, the *Francois Tixier's* engines were running, greatly increasing the difficulties for Coxswain Davies. Following the rescue, he was to be awarded the French Maritime Merit - the highest award given by the French for lifesaving at sea.

The 'Henry Blogg' going to the aid of the 'Francois Tixier' of Dunkirk, 8th July 1948. When taking off the crew, the French steamer capsized and pitched the remainder of the crew into the sea. All were picked up by the lifeboat. (P A Vicary)

Frequently the launching of the lifeboat is an operation combined with other services. September 11th 1948, saw one such service. The tug *Richard Lee Barber* of Great Yarmouth had tried to get alongside the French trawler *Georges Langanay* on the Haisbro' Sands. Being unsuccessful, the tug returned to Yarmouth for pumps and Cromer No 1 lifeboat launched at 11am. At 7pm the No 2 lifeboat was requested to launch with pumps; to be operated by three firemen. At 2am the following day the tug began towing but the vessel was not freed until 3pm. It was taken to Yarmouth harbour, the lifeboat taking a stern line for manoeuvring purposes. It was also one of the occasions that, with the vessel saved, the lifeboat crew were ale to enter a salvage claim.

NEW ERA - NEW BOATS

The years following the Second World War saw a change in the types of incidents with which the lifeboats dealt. The decrease in the number of sailing ships, improved navigation and the increase in pleasure boating led the RNLI to reconsider its strategy in the light of the ever growing costs of conventional lifeboats. The *Harriot Dixon* was replaced by the *William Henry and Mary King*, a 37ft Oakley class self-righting boat, in 1963. She was only to stay until 1967, as a review of records showed that over a period of ten years the No 2 boat had not been called on to back up No 1. As a

The 'Ruby and Arthur Reed' on Lifeboat Day, 1976. An Oakley class lifeboat, she served at Cromer for 20 years. (Poppyland Photos)

consequence, one of the new D-class fast Inshore Rescue Boats was stationed at Cromer. Introduced by the RNLI in 1963, such boats had proved their worth in dealing with the increasing number of small boat incidents.

Gas and oil exploration brought the rigs to the North Sea. The *Henry Blogg* launched on extended service when the rig *Sea Gem* collapsed on December 28th 1965, and on April 3rd of the following year damaged her steering when launching in heavy seas to go to the rig *Constellation.* The *Henry Blogg* went away for repairs, not to return. A reserve boat, the *Henry and Isabella Irwin,* filled the gap for a year before the arrival of the new 48ft 6in Oakley self-righting lifeboat *Ruby and Arthur Reed.* Presented by Mrs R M Reed of Eastbourne, the vessel was named on 2st June 1967. Costing £61,000, she had a 14ft beam, and with ballast and crew weighed 30 tons. Capable of 9.9 knots, she carried fuel for 273 nautical miles at full speed.

The *Ruby and Arthur Reed* was away for refit when on 15th November 1973 the trawler *Boston Jaguar* reported she had one man dead and an injured man, 37 miles NE by N of Cromer. The reserve lifeboat *Good Hope* launched at 23.12 hours and rendezvoused with the trawler at 02.30 at the Dudgeon light vessel. On board the lifeboat was Hon Secretary and Station Medical Officer Dr Paul Barclay, with first aider Richard Davies. Closing with the trawler, ropes were passed, but twice the lifeboat was knocked away.

The reserve lifeboat 'William Gammon' launching to the 'Diana V' on 30th September, 1978. (Poppyland Photos)

Against the coxswain's advice, Dr Barclay insisted on another try. With great skill 'Shrimp' Davies took the lifeboat alongside, enabling the doctor and first aider to board the trawler. In spite of his own considerable seasickness Dr Barclay tended his patient until they were both lifted off by helicopter at first light.

Dr Barclay was awarded the Bronze Medal of the Institution for gallantry. Coxswain 'Shrimp' Davies and Richard Davies both received the thanks of the Institution on Vellum.

'Shrimp' Davies was awarded the BEM in 1970, and was the subject of the television programme 'This is Your Life' in the year of his retirement, 1976. Richard Davies took over as coxswain. One of his first big tests came on November 14th 1977. The motor vessel *Nimrod* was making her way from Whitstable to Leith with a cargo of stone. With a 40 knot south-westerly wind, she developed a starboard list. Her 'Mayday' at 03.57 was heard by Cromer coastguard, who initiated rescue proceedings. The *Ruby and Arthur Reed* launched and the newly installed radar at Cromer coastguard lookout guided her to the search area. When the *Nimrod* sank, the Cromer lifeboat plucked her skipper from the sea, while the remainder of the crew were rescued by helicopter or other vessels in the area.

It was a reserve open Watson lifeboat, the *William Gammon,* that launched on 30th December 1978 into a very stormy sea and driving snow on her way to the listing *Diana V.* However, the distressed vessel was able to increase speed and make for the Humber and nine miles out the Cromer boat was recalled. Nearing the Humber, the *Diana V* faltered again and the Humber lifeboat went to her assistance, the coxswain being awarded a Silver Medal for gallantry. The Cromer crew took their boat into the shelter of Great Yarmouth harbour in the hours of darkness, and while not directly involved in assisting the *Diana V*, the night had been a severe test for the crew.

The ro-ro ferry *Ems* collided with the coaster *Undine* and sank on January 30th 1981. A major search operation involving a dozen ships resulted in 19 lives being saved, though four were lost. Cromer lifeboat was soon on the scene. The operation also involved two Sea King rescue helicopters from RAF Coltishall. These had replaced the Whirlwinds in 1980, greatly improving the capabilities of the sea rescue services.

However, helicopters have become casualties themselves, and the Cromer boat took part in the search following the crash of a Wessex helicopter in 1981. In fact, rescue work continues to be as busy as ever, because of the increase in the number of pleasure vessels at sea, combined with mishaps to aircraft and boats working with the gas rigs. In 1981 the *Ruby and Arthur*

The 'Ruby and Arthur Reed' returning from assisting an injured man on board the 'Heye P', July 27th, 1977. (Poppyland Photos)

Reed launched to the rig standby vessel *Cuttlefish,* aground on the Haisbro' Sands. The distressed vessel finally sank off Palling, but her crew were saved by helicopter and lifeboat. Coxswain Richard Davies had to cross the sands, touching bottom once, to take off the skipper and the cook. The decks of the *Cuttlefish* were awash and the stern under water as he carried out the rescue. Alongside these vessels which have made their appearance in the last 25 years there are still those of the traditional type; a coaster off Blakeney in August 1984, with her skipper requesting a doctor; local fishing boats in May 1985 requiring Cromer and Sheringham lifeboats to launch for escort duty. 'Shrimp' Davies became a crew member once again in September 1984, when Second Coxswain Billy Davies took the *Ruby and Arthur Reed* to a wrecked crab boat.

The year of 1978 had seen two members of the Inshore Lifeboat crew receive letters of thanks from RNLI headquarters for their efforts when a child was swept into the sea, and in 1981 a Bronze Medal was awarded to a helmsman of the inshore boat. The klaxon to assemble a crew was sounded on Friday May 1st; the crab boat *George William* had been swamped off East Runton and her crew were in the water. The lifeboat launched with Clive Rayment at the helm and crewmen Chris Craske and Frank Muirhead. The weather was fine, but a fresh to strong breeze meant working through

rolling surf and over an offshore bank with breaking seas at Runton. Rounding the capsized boat, and avoiding her debris, the two fishermen were taken into the boat and safely brought to the shore.
The first D-class Inshore Lifeboat (formerly called Inshore Rescue Boats) had served at Cromer from 1967 to 1972, and the second stayed until 1984. She was then replaced by D-307, named *Spirit of Round Table*. The boat was handed over by Mr M Downes of Sheringham and Cromer Round Table and dedicated in a service at the new east beach boathouse in August 1984. The west promenade had been the home of the inshore lifeboat "igloo" since the 1960s, but the state of the beach had made launching increasingly difficult and so the new boathouse was built back on the east side of the pier. The lifeboat served for ten years before she was replaced in turn by the current Inshore Lifeboat, *Chloe*.

RUBY AND ARTHUR REED II

In September 1982 the lifeboat *City of London* visited Cromer. She was the first of the new Tyne class, a type with a completely new hull design. She was travelling around the coast of the British Isles, visiting lifeboat stations where the boats are launched from slipways. Faster boats had been

The moment of anticipation, as the Cromer crew are ferried from the pier to the 'City of London', to test this new type of boat. September 1982. (Poppyland Photos)

The lifeboat 'City of London', the first of the Tyne class, at Cromer in September 1982, for evaluation by the Cromer crew (Poppyland Photos)

introduced where harbours were available, but the RNLI had been anxious to increase the speed of all its fleet. The initial reaction of the crew was favourable, but it was nearly two years before the second Tyne class lifeboat visited Cromer for slipway trials. The announcement was made that Cromer would receive a boat of this class and a local appeal towards the cost was launched. This would be combined with the legacy left by Mrs Ruby Reed to meet the £430,000 required.

The *Ruby and Arthur Reed* left the station for an overhaul several months before the new boat was due, and the *Guy and Clare Hunter,* formerly stationed at St Mary's, Isles of Scilly, took her place. She was an older type of boat of the Watson class, but was kept busy while at Cromer.

The 'Ruby and Arthur Reed II' at speed, her semi-planing hull lifting her in the water (Jim Bellingall)

The crew of the 'Ruby and Arthur Reed II', June 1986. (Poppyland Photos)

A crowded boathouse as HRH The Duke of Kent names and inspects the 'Ruby and Arthur Reed II' under the guidance of Coxswain Davies. (Poppyland Photos)

On September 15th 1985, both the Cromer lifeboats were launched to search for two missing divers. The Mundesley inshore rescue boat and a helicopter also put to sea. Second Coxswain Billy Davies, on the *Guy and Clare Hunter* felt that with a strong south-westerly breeze blowing and a moderate sea running Sheringham lifeboat should also assist, and it was from the *Manchester Unity of Oddfellows* that the missing divers were spotted. From the diving site two miles north of Overstrand, the ebb tide had carried them to West Runton in just over an hour. They were taken safely to Sheringham; Coxswain Jack West of Sheringham and Second Coxswain Billy Davies of Cromer both received letters of thanks from the chief of operations of the RNLI.

The *Ruby and Arthur Reed II,* the name chosen for the new Tyne class lifeboat, arrived on station on December 16th 1985, and it was not long before she was in action. On 24th January 1986, the 295-tonne Dutch fishing vessel *Jan Van Toon* struck the 76,000-tonne Greek tanker *Orleans* on her starboard side. Oil began to spill from the larger vessel, and a fire started on board. (The 295 tonne other vessel was hardly damaged!) The collision had occurred about 65 miles north-west of Cromer in force 10 northerly winds, and Cromer lifeboat launched about 15 minutes later. It took some three and a half hours in conditions varying from gale force 8, gusting to hurricane 12, for the lifeboat to reach the scene, probably the furthest the Cromer boat has ever travelled to a casualty. RAF helicopters, one of which had to make an emergency landing on a gas rig after a winch wire hit its rotor blades, had rescued the crew of the tanker, and the lifeboat commenced a stand-by duty until the *Orleans* was under tow. The occasion had been a severe and thorough test for boat and crew, and it was ten hours after launching that she gained the shelter of Great Yarmouth harbour. Following this service, a letter of appreciation was sent to Coxswain Richard Davies by the RNLI's chief of operations.

All this took place before the official naming ceremony and service of dedication. This was carried out on 20th June 1986, with the lifeboat being named by HRH the Duke of Kent, the President of the RNLI. As with some previous naming ceremonies, the sea conditions were not sufficiently good for the lifeboat to be launched! That is the way the announcement was made to the thousands of people gathered on the promenade, but of course the meaning is that the boat could not be re-housed if launched, and it remains a strict rule that she may only launch for emergency service under such circumstances. As with the service mentioned above, and as we mentioned earlier in the text, she has to make for Yarmouth harbour when such conditions prevail, and is brought back as soon as the sea state permits. In spite of the disappointment of no launch, all present enjoyed the day and Cromer was proud to have one of the new boats.

We have referred to the need for greater speed, and the Tyne class achieves 18 knots with the aid of a semi-planing hull. This helps the boat to rise higher in the water as it accelerates, thus reducing the drag. The extended bilge keels, particularly necessary for slipway launched boats, protect the propellers and enable the craft to operate in shallow waters. The watertight aluminium superstructure - the hull is steel - makes the boat self-righting, an operation which takes five seconds. The twin 425 hp engines are fed from two main tanks and a reserve, giving a range at full speed of 240 nautical miles. The displacement is 24 tons and the draught 4ft 2ins.

One of the most distinguished services to date of the *Ruby and Arthur Reed II* took place on 13th October 1993. The official report describes the launch as the roughest the station had experienced in the 30 years. Coxswain Richard Davies was awarded the Bronze Medal of the Lifeboat Institution, and Second Coxswain William Davies, mechanic Paul Wegg, crew members Robert Brownsell, Gary Humphrey and Paul Jeffries, together with head launcher John Lee, received bronze medal service certificates.

The lifeboat was launched in response to a call for help in the afternoon from the yacht *Happy Bear.* The 55 knot winds were pushing up a sea which was reaching the doors of the lifeboat house, and the lifeboat was buried in water as it launched. The lifeboat proceeded with great difficulty, sometimes becoming airborne as it took off from waves, crashing into the troughs. On finding the vessel, with gearbox difficulties, off Trimingham, the lifeboat commenced to escort the *Happy Bear* towards Great Yarmouth, and then succeeded in establishing a tow. Eventually second coxswain Davies jumped onto the yacht and helped to steer it into Yarmouth.

The final drama of 1993 did not involve the launch of the lifeboat, but certainly gave a new challenge to the crew. A service barge broke free from its mooring off Runton, and broke through the pier at the promenade end. For several weeks the crew had to negotiate a fragile bridge to reach the main pier and lifeboat, until repairs were completed!

Much has changed, but the RNLI continues to rely totally on voluntary contributions. Hundreds of unpaid and unrecognised hours are put in every year by crews, wives, helpers and fund-raisers. In Cromer the guides and attendants of the Lifeboat Museum and the pier boathouse now raise thousands of pounds annually for the Institution. The Branch Lifeboat Committee guides station activities, while the Ladies' Guild arrange events throughout the year in support of the boats. Finally, Cromer has been fortunate in having a dedicated and capable succession of Honorary Secretaries, the men who over the years have been responsible for the smooth operation of the Cromer Lifeboat Station.